Sew Mary!

If you love the look of Mary Engelbreit's magical artwork and the feel of fabric accessories, then you're in for a treat. We've fashioned more than 20 simple sewing projects, dolled them up with very "Mary" fabrics, and added the most enchanting embellishments — with irresistible results! From whimsical wearables to flourishes for the home, these adorable accents are simply delightful.

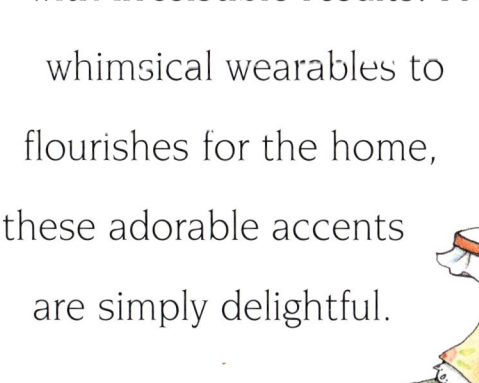

Photo by Rich Saal

Growing up in St. Louis, Missouri, Mary Engelbreit adored drawing. She began sketching as soon as she could hold a crayon, and by the age of 11 she knew without a doubt that she wanted to grow up to be an artist.

After short-lived careers at an art store, an ad agency, and the *St. Louis Post-Dispatch*, Mary began illustrating fantasy greeting cards. But she really found her niche after her first son was born, when her artistic focus turned to more "everyday" moments.

Now an internationally known artist, Mary has created more than 4,000 images featuring whimsical quotes, precocious children, and, of course, her trademark cherries and Scottie dogs. In Mary's lovely, nostalgic world, life is richly detailed and "to imagine is everything!"

Table of Contents

Just for You

Book Cover	6
Bookmark	7
Dream Pillow	8
Accessory Bag	10

 ## What to Wear

Straw Hat	14
Vest	15
Embellished Jacket	16
Heart Pins	18

Bags to Carry

Book Bag	22
Jewelry Pouch	23
Scottie Backpack	25
Cell Phone Bag	26
Purse	27

 ## Me & My Home

Heart Pillow	32
Bolster Pillow	33
Chair Cover	34
Table Skirt	36
Wall Hanging	37
Looped Rug	38

Just for You

Indulge yourself with pretty and practical knickknacks made from very "Mary" fabric! You'll simply adore our buttoned-up book cover, playful page keeper, lovely accessory bag, and dreamy pillow.

Book Cover

You will need a hardback book, Mary Engelbreit yellow garden fabric (amount will depend on size of book; see Step 5), green print fabric (amount will depend on size of book; see Step 2), fusible interfacing, red rickrack, two 3/4" dia. red buttons, black beading cord elastic, liquid fray preventative, and fabric glue.

Match right sides and use a 1/4" seam allowance for all sewing unless otherwise indicated.

1. Read **General Instructions**, pages 42-44.
2. On wrong side of green fabric, lay opened book. Trace lightly around book with a pencil. Remove book. Measure and mark 1/2" outside top and bottom lines. Measure and mark 5 1/2" from each side line. Cut out along outside lines. Cut a piece of interfacing the same size.
3. Iron fusible interfacing to back of green fabric.
4. Press top and bottom edges of green fabric 1/2" to wrong side; press side edges 1/4" to wrong side. Press side edges again 5 1/4" to *right* side; sew in place along top and bottom edges. Turn right side out.

5. To make yellow flap, measure thickness of book; add desired measurements for front and back overlap plus ¾" for seam allowances to get width measurement. (Our book is 1" thick; we added 2½" overlap on the front and 1½" overlap on the back.) Measure height of book; add ½" for seam allowances to get height measurement. Cut two pieces of yellow fabric and one piece of interfacing the determined measurements.
6. Iron fusible interfacing to back of one yellow fabric piece. Leaving an opening for turning, sew yellow fabric pieces together along all edges. Clip corners, turn, and hand sew opening closed.
7. Wrap yellow flap around book as desired. Press height edge at back ¼" to one side. Place pressed edge of flap at desired overlap on back of book cover. Being careful to sew through only one layer of book cover, hand sew in place.
8. On remaining height edge of flap, glue a length of rickrack to the underside so that half of rickrack extends past the edge of the flap as shown in photo. Use liquid fray preventative on cut ends of rickrack.
9. Cut a 3" length of elastic. Knot ends together to form a loop. Sew a button to flap as shown in photo, catching ends of elastic loop between button and flap.
10. Place book cover on book. Fold flap onto front cover; mark placement of remaining button on green fabric so that elastic loop will be slightly stretched. Remove book. Being careful to sew through only one layer of book cover, sew remaining button to book cover front.
11. Replace book in cover; fold flap and loop elastic over button to close.

Bookmark

You will need ⅛ yd Mary Engelbreit print fabric, ¼ yd of ⅛"w black satin ribbon, ¼ yd of 1"w black and white checked ribbon, liquid fray preventative, polyester fiberfill, and fabric glue.

Match right sides and use a ¼" seam allowance for all sewing unless otherwise indicated.

1. Read **General Instructions**, pages 42-44.
2. Leaving a ¼" seam allowance all the way around, cut two "Here" hearts from motto fabric. Leaving an opening for turning, sew hearts together. Clip curves and turn. Stuff heart with polyester fiberfill; hand sew opening closed.
3. Cut 8½" lengths of satin and checked ribbon. Use liquid fray preventative on cut ends of both ribbons. Fold one end of checked ribbon ¼" to wrong side; glue. On remaining end, fold corners to center to form a point; tuck one end of satin ribbon in point and glue.
4. Knot remaining end of satin ribbon. Hand sew knot to top of stuffed heart.

Dream Pillow

You will need 3/8 yd yellow print fabric; 1/3 yd Mary Engelbreit blue cherry fabric; 1/8 yd green print fabric; red and green felt; string; thumbtack; freezer paper; 1/2 yd of 1/4"w red satin ribbon; 1" dia. yellow button; red, green, and yellow embroidery floss; pinking shears; potpourri; and a 12" x 15" pillow form.

Match right sides and use a 1/2" seam allowance for all sewing unless otherwise indicated.

1. Read **General Instructions**, pages 42-44.
2. Cut a 12 1/2" x 25" rectangle from yellow fabric. Cut a 9 1/2" x 25" rectangle from blue fabric. Aligning one long edge, sew rectangles together.
3. Press remaining long raw edge of blue fabric 1/2" to wrong side.
4. Fold sewn piece in half widthwise and sew along short edge of yellow fabric and adjoining long pieced edge.
5. With wrong sides together, fold blue fabric in half to meet seam on wrong side. Topstitch in place 1/4" from seam. Turn right side out.
6. Trace two of each pattern piece, below, onto freezer paper. Iron shiny side of freezer paper pattern to felt with warm iron. Cut out felt along outside pattern lines. Backstitch vein lines on one leaf set with green floss. Remove freezer paper.
7. Blanket stitch leaf pieces together with green floss. Blanket stitch flower pieces together with red floss. Stitching only through back flower, hand sew leaves to back of flower pieces.
8. Arrange flower on pillowcase as shown in photo. Sew button to pillowcase through center of flower with yellow floss.
9. To make sachet, cut a 7" square from green fabric. Refer to **Cutting a Fabric Circle**, page 43, and use a 3 1/4" length of string to cut circle with pinking shears.
10. Leaving thread ends loose, sew a running stitch 1/4" from edge of circle. Place potpourri in center of circle. Pull ends of thread to gather; knot tightly and trim.
11. Tie ribbon into a bow around sachet. Place one loop of bow around button to attach sachet to pillow.
12. Insert pillow form.

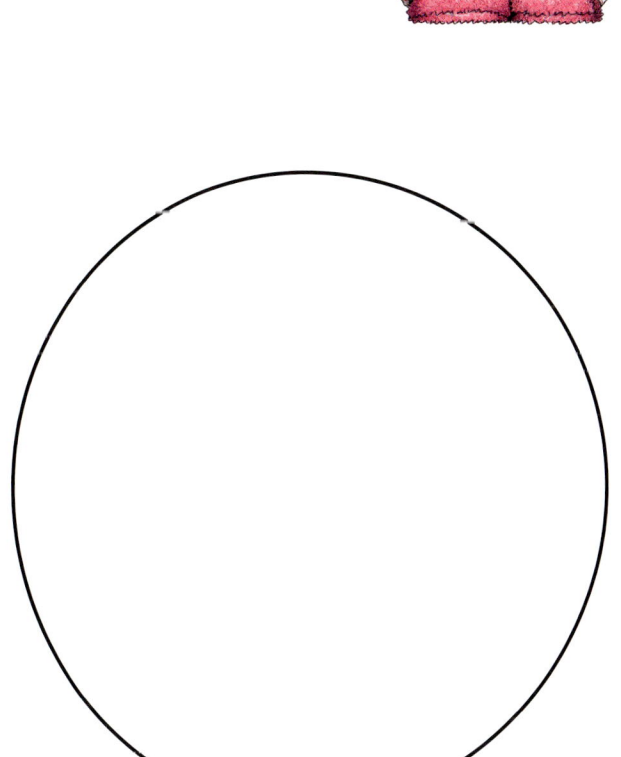

Mary Engelbreit Enterprises, Inc., and Leisure Arts, Inc., grant permission to the owner of this book to copy or trace the patterns on this page for personal use only.

Accessory Bag

You will need ²⁄₃ yd Mary Engelbreit yellow cherry fabric, ¹⁄₄ yd Mary Engelbreit blue cherry fabric, ¹⁄₃ yd Mary Engelbreit floral fabric, ¹⁄₂ yd Mary Engelbreit blue and black checked fabric, 5 yds of ³⁄₁₆" dia. red cording, 5 yds of ¹⁄₈"w black trim, eleven ⁵⁄₈" dia. red dome buttons, 1 yd black beading cord elastic, ⁷⁄₈ yd of ³⁄₈"w green satin ribbon, green embroidery floss, fusible interfacing, ¹⁄₄" dia. gold grommet, triangular wire clothes hanger 4³⁄₄" tall from base of hook to bottom, and fabric glue.

Match right sides and use a ¹⁄₂" seam allowance for all sewing unless otherwise indicated.

1. Read **General Instructions**, pages 42-44.
2. Cut one 22" x 42¹⁄₂" rectangle from yellow fabric and fusible interfacing. Iron interfacing to back of fabric.
3. Press all raw edges of fabric ¹⁄₂" to wrong side twice; topstitch.
4. Fold top edge of fabric 5¹⁄₂" to wrong side; press. Unfold fabric and attach grommet in center of fold line.

10

5. Refold fabric with right sides together; insert wire hanger through grommet. Lightly mark angle lines of hanger with a pencil (**Fig. 1**).

   Fig. 1

6. Remove hanger; sew along marked lines. Trim excess fabric 1/4" from lines. Turn bag right side out.
7. Cut one 2" x 20½" strip of checked fabric for bottom binding. Press one long edge of strip ½" to wrong side.
8. Matching right sides and raw edges, sew binding strip to bottom edge of fabric. Wrap and pin pressed edge of binding to back just past stitching. Sew along front seam line to secure binding on back side. Trim ends of binding even with yellow fabric.
9. Cut two 2" x 11½" strips of checked fabric for top bindings. Press one end of each strip ½" to wrong side; topstitch. Press one long edge of each strip ½" to wrong side.
10. Placing topstitched ends next to grommet, follow Step 8 to attach bindings to top edges of fabric.
11. Cut two 2" x 30½" strips of checked fabric for side bindings. Press ends of strips ½" to wrong side; topstitch. Press one long edge of each strip ½" to wrong side. Covering raw ends of top and bottom bindings, follow Step 8 to attach bindings to side edges of fabric.
12. To make pockets, cut a 7" x 23" strip from blue cherry fabric and fusible interfacing. Cut two 5" x 29" strips from checked fabric and fusible interfacing. Cut one 10" x 29" strip from floral fabric and fusible interfacing. Iron fusible interfacing to wrong side of each fabric strip. Press raw edges of fabric strips ¼" to wrong side twice; topstitch.

13. Press 1½" pleats on each end of cherry pocket. Press pleats in remaining pockets as shown (**Fig. 2**).

    Fig. 2

    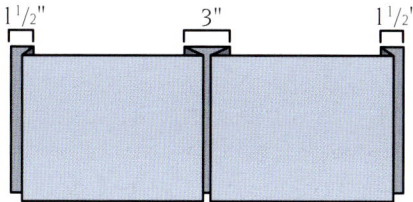

14. Evenly space three buttons along top edge of cherry pocket; sew in place. Sew one button to center of each remaining pocket between pleats.
15. Pin floral pocket to yellow fabric 2" from bottom. Topstitch in place along center pleat, sides, and bottom.
16. Repeat to sew checked pockets to yellow fabric above floral pocket, spacing each 1" above previous.
17. Pin cherry pocket to yellow fabric 1" above top checked pocket. Topstitch in place along sides and bottom.
18. Glue trim along bottom of each pocket. Glue cording above trim.
19. Glue trim along binding. Glue cording over seam between binding and trim.
20. For ribbon leaves, cut ten 3" lengths of ribbon. Overlap ends of each ribbon at center; knot floss around centers.
21. Cut nine 3" lengths of elastic. Wrap one length around each sewn button, with ends extending above pocket; tack in place on accessory bag. Glue ribbon leaf sets on top of elastic ends.
22. Cut one 7" length of elastic. Thread each end through one button and knot. Sew buttons 3" from grommet and 1½" apart on yellow fabric. Insert hanger through grommet, catching elastic behind hanger. Glue remaining ribbon leaf set to elastic 1" below grommet.

What to Wear

The age-old question of "what to wear" won't be a problem anymore, thanks to our darling straw hat, jaunty collared jacket, pretty patchwork vest, and charming heart-shaped pins. How precious!

Straw Hat

You will need a straw hat, 1/4 yd black and white striped fabric, 1/8 yd green print fabric, 1/8 yd *each* of four different fabrics for flowers, five 3/4" dia. buttons from covered button kits, batting, freezer paper, and a hot glue gun.

Match right sides and use a 1/2" seam allowance for all sewing unless otherwise indicated.

1. Read **General Instructions**, pages 42-44.
2. To make bow, cut an 8" x 27" strip of striped fabric. Fold strip in half lengthwise. Fold in half widthwise and trim ends at an angle; unfold widthwise.
3. Leaving an opening for turning, sew all raw edges of strip together. Clip corners and turn right side out; press. Hand sew opening closed. Tie into a bow.

4. To make hatband, measure around the crown of your hat; add 1". Cut a 6" wide strip of striped fabric the determined measurement. Fold strip in half lengthwise; sew long raw edges together and turn.
5. Using patterns on page 19, refer to **Making Shapes**, page 43, to make one small flower and leaf set, three medium flower and leaf sets, and one large flower and leaf set.
6. Cover buttons with scraps of fabric that will contrast with corresponding flowers. Sew buttons to flower centers. Hot glue a leaf set to the back of each flower.
7. Wrap hatband around crown of hat; overlap ends in back and hot glue in place. Hot glue bow to back of hat at crown. Hot glue small flower to brim of hat beneath knot of bow. Hot glue one medium flower on crown of hat above knot of bow. Arrange and hot glue remaining flowers to crown of hat along hatband.

Vest

You will need a denim vest; Mary Engelbreit yellow floral and black cherry fabric; red polka-dot fabric (amount of all these fabrics will depend on vest size; see Steps 2-3); 1/8 yd green print fabric; 1/8 yd yellow checked fabric; 1/8 yd solid red fabric; red, yellow, and green thread; 3/8"w black and white checked ribbon; 1/4"w black and white checked ribbon; red jumbo rickrack; 1/2"w lace trim; 5/8" dia. red shank-style button; assorted beads; charm; toggle clasp; clear nylon thread; tracing paper; transfer paper; and paper-backed fusible web.

1. Read **General Instructions**, pages 42-44.
2. Lay tracing paper over one side of vest front; trace outside edges. Remove from vest. Draw diagonal lines to divide vest into three sections as shown in photo. Cut out each section for patterns.
3. Adding 1/2" to each side as you go, use section patterns to cut one piece from floral, cherry, and polka-dot fabric. Turn patterns over and cut another piece from each fabric for opposite side of vest.
4. Press edges of each fabric piece 1/2" to wrong side. Butting edges together, pin fabric pieces to front of vest. Topstitch in place 1/4" from outside edges of vest. Where fabrics butt together, layer rickrack and 1/4" ribbon together or lace trim and 3/8" ribbon together; topstitch in place with clear nylon thread.
5. Measure width of vest at shoulder seam. Divide this number by 3.25, then multiply by 100. Enlarge the flower pattern on page 40 by this percentage on a photocopier. Refer to **Preparing Fusible Appliqués**, page 42, to make two solid red flowers with checked centers, two checked flowers with solid red centers, and four two-leaf sets.
6. Arrange and fuse flowers to vest as shown in photo. Refer to **Machine Satin Stitching**, page 42, to satin stitch around each flower piece with matching thread. Satin stitch leaves and veins with green thread.
7. Sew button to one side of vest and circle part of toggle clasp to other side. Use a doubled length of thread and bring your needle up alongside the button. Thread beads, charm, and more beads as desired onto thread. Add bar part of toggle clasp onto end of thread. Take needle back through all beads and secure thread beneath button.

Embellished Jacket

You will need a jacket with stand-up collar, 1/4 yd Mary Engelbreit yellow Scottie fabric, black and white striped fabric (amount will depend on jacket size; see Steps 5, 8, and 13), 1/4 yd solid black fabric, 1/8 yd red polka-dot fabric, scrap of solid pink fabric, red mini rickrack, 3/8 yd of 3/8"w yellow satin ribbon, 5/8 yd of 7/8"w black polka-dot ribbon, 1/8" dia. red cording, two 1/4" dia. black buttons, black thread, red buttons (optional), large snap, white acrylic paint, paintbrush, fusible interfacing, paper-backed fusible web, tracing paper, and fabric glue.

Match right sides and use a 1/2" seam allowance for all sewing unless otherwise indicated.

1. Read **General Instructions**, pages 42-44.
2. To make collar, lay jacket with collar flat. Lay tracing paper over collar. Trace bottom seam of collar; mark placement of seams on shoulders. Remove tracing paper. Mark another line 3 1/2" out from collar line; extend shoulder seam lines to meet this line. Draw a curve to connect ends of collar line and outside line. Cut along each drawn line to make three collar patterns.
3. Adding 1/2" to each side as you go, cut one of each collar pattern from Scottie fabric for top of collar. Turn patterns over and repeat for bottom of collar.
4. Sew top collar pieces together along shoulder lines; repeat with bottom collar pieces. Cut fusible interfacing the same size as top collar; iron to wrong side of top collar.
5. For ruffle, measure around outside edge of collar; multiply by two. Cut a 3" wide strip of striped fabric the determined measurement. Matching wrong sides, press strip in half lengthwise.
6. Baste 3/8" and 1/4" from raw edges of ruffle. Pull basting threads to gather ruffle to fit outside edge of top collar, distributing gathers evenly. Bend ends of ruffle so that raw edges on ends will not show; baste in place.
7. Leaving an opening for turning, sew top collar to bottom collar. Clip curves, turn, and hand sew opening closed. Glue rickrack along outside edge of collar; sew snap pieces to opposite ends of collar. Cut a 19" length of polka-dot ribbon; tie in a bow and sew to collar front.
8. To make jacket trim, rip out bottom hem of jacket; press. Measure length of one side of bottom hem from front placket to side seam. Cut a 4" wide piece of striped fabric this length plus 1 1/4". Repeat to measure and cut fabric for remaining front hem. Measure length of back hem from side seam to side seam, add 1", and cut fabric for back hem.
9. Sew fabric pieces together along short sides to wrap around jacket. Press short ends 1/4" to wrong side. Baste cording along one long edge.
10. Center jacket on trim; sew in place. Turn jacket trim to right side of jacket; topstitch in place along cording. Wrap ends of jacket trim around placket of jacket front; whipstitch in place.
11. Use pattern on page 28 and refer to Steps 1 and 2 of **Preparing Fusible Appliqués**, page 42, to make Scottie dog appliqué pieces using solid black, red polka-dot, and pink fabrics. Turn tracing paper over and repeat to make a reversed Scottie dog.
12. Center and fuse appliqué pieces to each side of jacket front with Scottie dogs facing. Refer to **Machine Satin Stitching**, page 42, to satin stitch around all raw edges of appliqués with black thread. Use end of paintbrush to make two white dots on each black button. Sew black buttons in place for eyes. Cut two 6" lengths of yellow ribbon. Tie each length in a bow; glue one to neck of each Scottie dog.
13. To make cuffs, remove jacket cuffs and press sleeves. Measure width of cuffs; multiply by two and add 1". Measure length of cuffs; add 1". Cut two pieces of striped fabric the determined measurements.
14. Sew cording to one long edge (length) of each piece of cuff fabric. Press remaining long edge 1/2" to wrong side.
15. Pin each cuff in place around end of sleeve with cording next to raw edge of sleeve. Topstitch along cording. Fold bottom of cuff up to meet cording, right sides together. Sew along each short end; clip corners and turn. Whipstitch remaining side of cuff to the inside sleeve.
16. If desired, replace buttons of jacket with red buttons.

Heart Pins

For each pin, you will need a scrap of fabric, 3/4" dia. button, 3/8" dia. button, 10/0 black and white seed beads, 8/0 black and white seed beads, 1/3 yd of 3/8"w polka-dot grosgrain ribbon, polyester fiberfill, pin back clasp, charm, heavy-duty thread to match fabric, black thread, tracing paper, and fabric glue.

1. Read **General Instructions**, pages 42-44.
2. Trace heart pattern, page 19, onto tracing paper; cut out. Use pattern to cut two hearts from fabric.
3. Cut 3 1/2" of ribbon for bow hanger. Fold in half; pin cut ends to the top center of one heart. Matching right sides, leaving an opening for turning, and being careful not to catch fold of bow hanger in seam, use a 1/4" seam allowance to sew hearts together.
4. Turn heart right side out. Stuff heart with fiberfill; hand sew opening closed. 
5. Stack small button on large button; sew to center of heart.
6. Cut a 12" length of heavy-duty thread; knot end. Insert needle into back of heart, coming up at center top seam. When knot catches on fabric, give thread a quick, short pull to "pop" knot through fabric into fiberfill. Alternating colors, thread four 10/0 beads onto thread. Align beads with seam of heart; take a small stitch through heart to anchor. Take thread back through 4th bead again, then string another four beads. Repeat to attach beads along seam to bottom point of heart.
7. At point, add three beads, alternating colors, and charm. Sew back through three beads and stitch through point of heart to anchor. Continue threading beads around heart until you reach the top.
8. Repeat Step 6 to attach 8/0 beads around large button.

9. Cut 4" of ribbon for bow. Glue ends together to form a loop. Cut 3 1/2" of ribbon for bow tails; fold as shown (**Fig. 1**), then glue in place. Place point of bow tails at center of bow. Insert pieces through hanger (**Fig. 2**); tightly wrap and knot black thread around hanger just beneath bow to cinch. Tack pin back clasp to back of bow.

Fig. 1

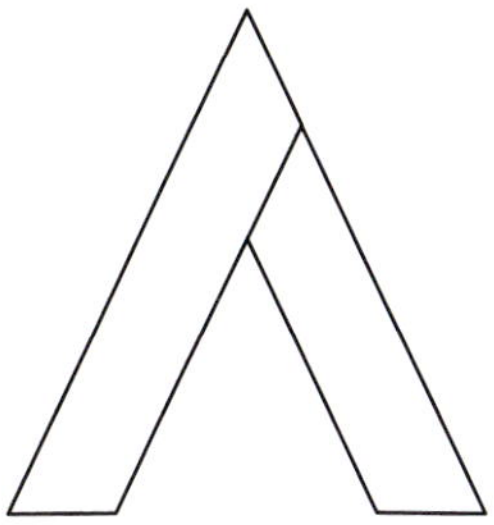

Fig. 2

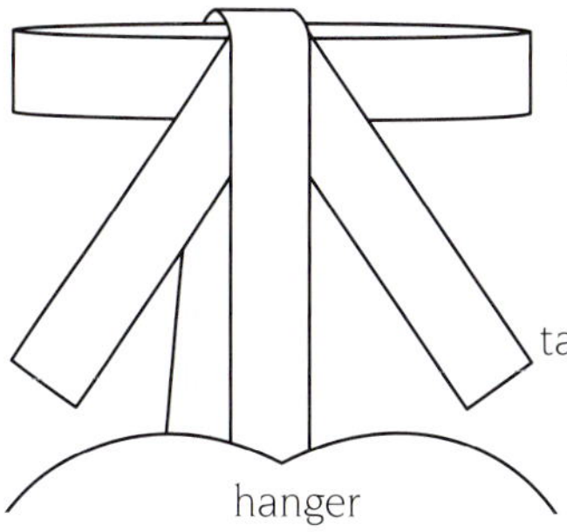

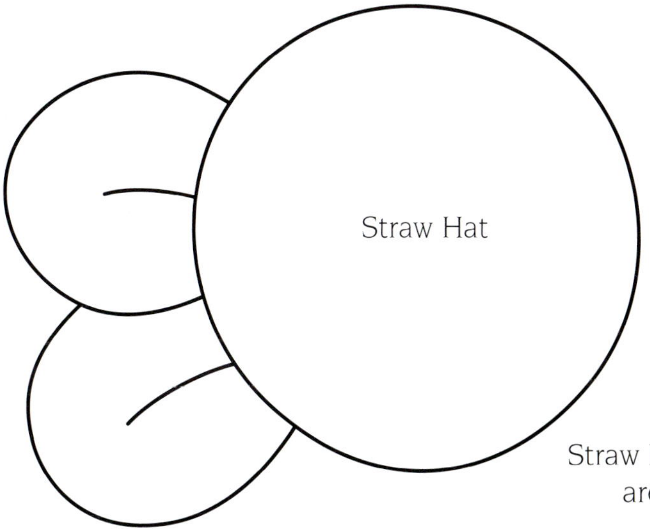

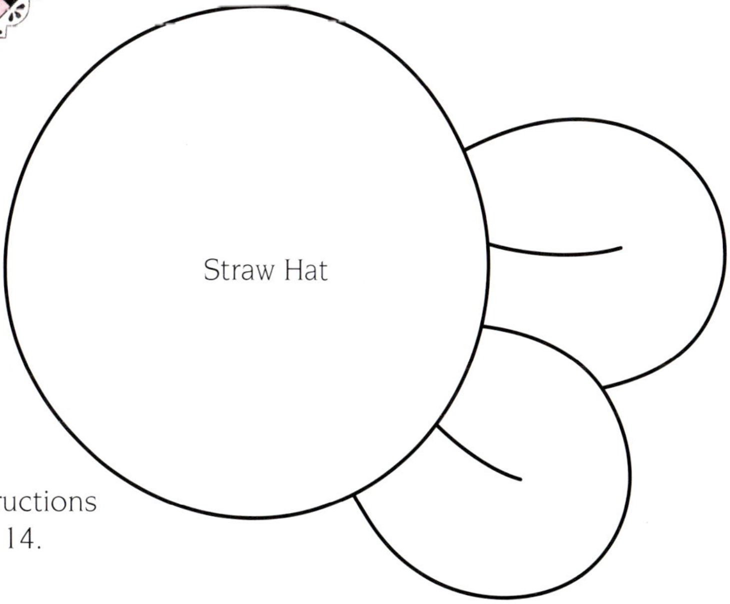

bow

tails

hanger

Heart Pins

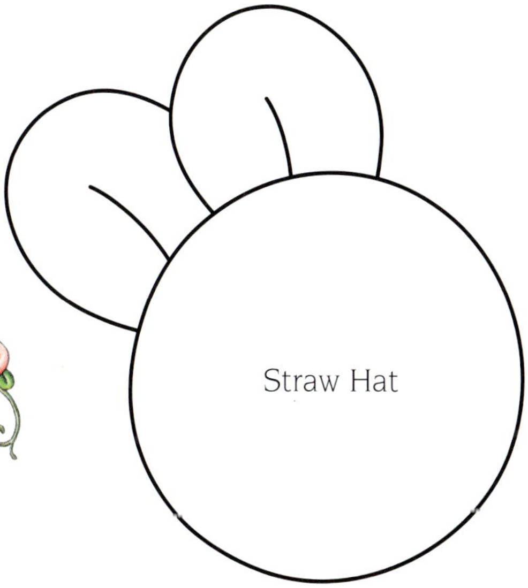

Straw Hat

Straw Hat

Straw Hat

Straw Hat instructions are on pg. 14.

Mary Engelbreit Enterprises, Inc., and Leisure Arts, Inc., grant permission to the owner of this book to copy or trace the patterns on this page for personal use only.

Bags to Carry

Every woman knows that the right bag is more than just an accessory — it's a necessity! That's why we've included patterns for five bags of all shapes and sizes; they embody all the magic of Mary's drawings and hold everything from books to baubles!

Book Bag

You will need 1/3 yd black checked fabric, 1/2 yd red polka-dot fabric, 1/4 yd blue print fabric, 1/8 yd green print fabric, scrap of yellow print fabric, 7/8" dia. button from covered button kit, two 3/4" dia. black buttons, fusible interfacing, freezer paper, scraps of batting, and fabric glue.

Match right sides and use a 1/2" seam allowance for all sewing unless otherwise indicated.

1. Read **General Instructions**, pages 42-44.
2. Cut two 10" x 12 1/2" rectangles from checked fabric and fusible interfacing. Iron interfacing to wrong side of fabric rectangles.
3. For pocket, cut a 6 1/2" x 6 3/4" rectangle from blue fabric. Press each edge 1/4" to wrong side twice. Topstitch one short edge for top of pocket. Pin pocket on right side of one checked rectangle with top edge 3" from one end and centered horizontally. Topstitch sides and bottom. To make pen holder, measure 1 1/2" from right side of pocket and topstitch down pocket.
4. Sew checked rectangles together along side and bottom edges. For each bottom corner, match side seam to bottom seam to form a point. Sew across each point 1 1/4" from end (**Fig. 1**). Turn bag right side out.

Fig. 1

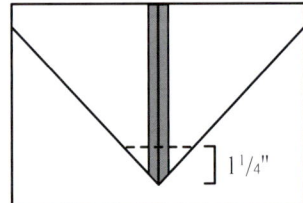

5. To make lining, cut two 10" x 14" rectangles from polka-dot fabric. Repeat Step 4 with polka-dot rectangles. Press top raw edge of lining 1/2" to wrong side.

6. With lining wrong side out, slip lining inside book bag. Fold top of lining over top of book bag; topstitch.
7. To make handle, cut a 4" x 24" strip from polka-dot fabric and batting. Pin batting on wrong side of fabric; fold fabric and batting in half, matching long edges. Sew one short end and long raw edges; clip corners and turn handle right side out. Hand sew remaining short end closed.
8. Sew handle to each side of book bag with a black button.
9. Use pattern on page 28 and refer to **Making Shapes**, page 43, to make one red flower and three green leaves. Cover button with yellow fabric; sew to center of flower. Arrange flower and leaves on pocket as shown; glue in place.

Jewelry Pouch

You will need 1/4 yd solid pink fabric, 1/8 yd green print fabric, 1/8 yd yellow checked fabric, pink and green thread, paper-backed fusible web, freezer paper, tracing paper, transfer paper, batting, and 5/8" dia. adhesive hook-and-loop fastener dot.

Match right sides and use a 1/4" seam allowance for all sewing unless otherwise indicated.

1. Read **General Instructions**, pages 42-44.
2. Trace leaf patterns on page 29 onto freezer paper. For each freezer paper pattern, cut two squares of green fabric and one square of batting large enough to fit pattern. Iron shiny side of freezer paper pattern to wrong side of one fabric square with warm iron. With pattern on top, layer fabric squares, right sides together, on batting.
3. Machine stitch around freezer paper pattern, leaving end of leaf open. Trim fabric and batting to 1/4" from end and stitching. Remove freezer paper, clip curves, and turn. Refer to **Machine Satin Stitching**, page 42, to satin stitch vein lines with green thread.
4. Refer to **Preparing Fusible Appliqués**, page 42, and use pattern on page 29 to make one yellow flower center.
5. Trace all lines of flower pattern, page 29, onto tracing paper; cut out. Cut four pink flowers. On right side of one flower, place transfer paper, coated side down. Place tracing paper pattern over transfer paper and draw over detail lines with a ballpoint pen that does not write or a dull pencil.
6. Fuse yellow flower center in place on this flower. Machine satin stitch transferred embellishment lines with pink thread.
7. Leaving an opening for turning, sew satin stitched flower to one plain flower. Clip curves and turn; hand sew opening closed. Repeat to sew remaining two flower pieces together.
8. Using placement lines on pattern, pin leaf sets to outside edge of one flower set with points of leaves toward the center. Leaving 3" open between leaves, place remaining flower set on top and sew pieces together. Clip curves and turn.
9. Attach hook and loop fastener dot to open edge of flower.

Scottie Backpack

You will need 1/2 yd Mary Engelbreit yellow Scottie fabric, 1/4 yd Mary Engelbreit black cherry fabric, 1/4 yd solid black fabric, 1/2 yd lining fabric, scraps of red polka-dot and pink solid fabric, black thread, 1/2 yd batting, 7/8 yd red jumbo rickrack, 2 yds of 1"w black grosgrain ribbon, 1/4" dia. black button, paper-backed fusible web, tracing paper, white acrylic paint, and a paintbrush.

Match right sides and use a 1/2" seam allowance for all sewing unless otherwise indicated.

1. Read **General Instructions**, pages 42-44.
2. Use pattern on page 28 and refer to Steps 1 and 2 of **Preparing Fusible Appliqués**, page 42, to make Scottie dog appliqué pieces using solid black, red polka-dot, and pink fabrics. Remove paper backing from appliqués.
3. Cut a 14 1/2" x 27" rectangle from yellow fabric. Matching wrong sides, fold in half widthwise; center and fuse appliqué pieces to fabric. Unfold and refer to **Machine Satin Stitching**, page 42, to satin stitch around all raw edges of appliqués with black thread. Use end of paintbrush to make two white dots on button. Sew button in place for eye.
4. Cut two 6" x 14 1/2" rectangles from black fabric. Sew one black rectangle to each short end of yellow rectangle to make backpack. Cut two 14 1/2" lengths of rickrack; sew one length along each seam.
5. Cut one 14 1/2" x 34" rectangle from batting and lining fabric. Fold both pieces in half widthwise; insert lining into batting. Sew along each long side. Trim batting and fabric close to seam.
6. Refold backpack in half widthwise. Measure 1 1/2" from short ends and mark a 1" opening with pins. Cut two 34" lengths of ribbon. Insert one length of ribbon 1/2" into each side of fold at bottom of backpack. Catching ribbon at fold and leaving space between pins open, sew along each long side. Turn backpack right side out.
7. Insert batting and lining into backpack.
8. Press top edge of backpack 1/4" to wrong side. Press again 1 1/4" to wrong side; topstitch.
9. Bring remaining ends of ribbon to top of backpack and thread through openings. Thread one ribbon to front and one to back, bringing ribbon ends out through opposite opening. Topstitch ribbon ends just inside casing.

Cell Phone Bag

You will need 1/8 yd Mary Engelbreit floral fabric, 1/8 yd Mary Engelbreit print fabric, 1/8 yd batting, paper-backed fusible web, 7/8 yd of 1/8" dia. black satin cord, and 5/8" dia. adhesive hook-and-loop fastener dot.

Match right sides and use a 1/2" seam allowance for all sewing unless otherwise indicated.

1. Read **General Instructions**, pages 42-44.
2. Cut two 4" x 17" rectangles of floral fabric and one 4" x 17" rectangle of batting. Match right sides of fabric and stack batting on top. Leaving opening for turning, sew around outside edges of rectangle. Clip corners, turn right side out, and hand sew opening closed.
3. Fold one short end of sewn fabric 6" to top; pin in place. Pleat folded edge into side seams about 1" (**Fig. 1**). Using a 1/8" seam allowance, sew side seams.

   Fig. 1

   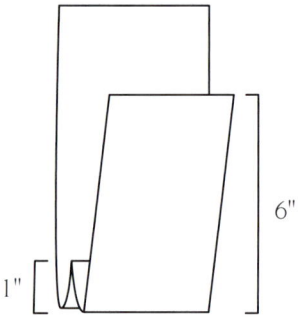

4. Knot ends of satin cord; hand sew one end to each side of bag at seam. Turn bag right side out. Whipstitch edges of flap 1/8" to wrong side.
5. Leaving 1/4" seam allowance all the way around, cut "Miss Smarty" from motto fabric. Press each edge 1/4" to wrong side. Cut a piece of fusible web the same size; iron fusible web to back of motto. Remove paper backing; fuse onto flap. Topstitch along folded edges of motto.
6. Attach fastener dot pieces to inside of flap and outside of bag beneath flap.

Purse

You will need ¹⁄₄ yd Mary Engelbreit black cherry fabric; ⁵⁄₈ yd black and white striped fabric; ²⁄₃ yd red polka-dot fabric; 1⅝ yds of ⅛" dia. cotton cord; black elastic cord; black beading cord; 3" x 10" cardboard; craft glue; two ¼" dia. silver grommets; 1⅛" dia. black button; ⅝" dia. red shank-style button; bead mix, including glass cherry beads; fabric glue; iron-on stabilizer; and a hot glue gun.

Match right sides and use a ½" seam allowance for all sewing unless otherwise indicated.

1. Read **General Instructions**, pages 42-44.
2. To make bias welting, cut a 12" square of polka-dot fabric. Refer to **Making Bias Strips**, page 43, to make a 2⅜" wide bias strip. Center cotton cord on wrong side of bias strip. Matching long edges, fold bias strip over cotton cord. Using zipper foot, baste next to cotton cord to make welting.
3. With stripe parallel to long edge, cut one 11" x 18" rectangle from striped fabric for purse body. With stripe parallel to long edge, cut two 4" x 8" rectangles from striped fabric for gussets.
4. Cut two 18" lengths of welting; baste to each long edge of purse body.
5. Make a ¼" diagonal clip on both corners of one short end of gusset. Folding purse body around clipped end, pin body to gusset. Sew in place. (**Fig. 1**).

Fig. 1

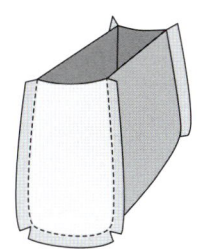

6. Repeat to sew remaining long edge of purse body to remaining gusset. Turn purse right side out.
7. Press top raw edge of purse ½" to wrong side.
8. Using polka-dot fabric, repeat Steps 3, 5, and 6 to make lining; do not turn right side out.
9. Cut one 6½" x 11" rectangle from cherry and polka-dot fabrics for flap; use a dinner plate to round corners on one long edge of each rectangle. Baste remaining welting to curved edge of cherry flap. Fold a 4" length of elastic cord in half and baste to center top of curved edge of flap. Fuse stabilizer to polka-dot flap. Sew cherry flap to polka-dot flap along curved edge. Turn flap right side out.

10. Insert polka-dot lining in purse. Insert straight edge of flap between purse and lining along one long edge; topstitch along top edge of purse.
11. Fold flap to front of purse; sew black button in place so that elastic will loop around it. Clip shank from red button; hot glue red button to black button.
12. Attach a grommet near top on each side of purse.
13. Cut one 58" length of beading cord; thread cord through one grommet. Thread beads randomly onto both cord ends. Thread end of cord through remaining grommet and knot to other cord end.
14. Draw around cardboard on wrong side of polka-dot fabric. Cut out fabric 1" outside drawn lines. Wrapping and gluing edges to back, fold fabric around cardboard like a package. Insert cardboard in bottom of purse.

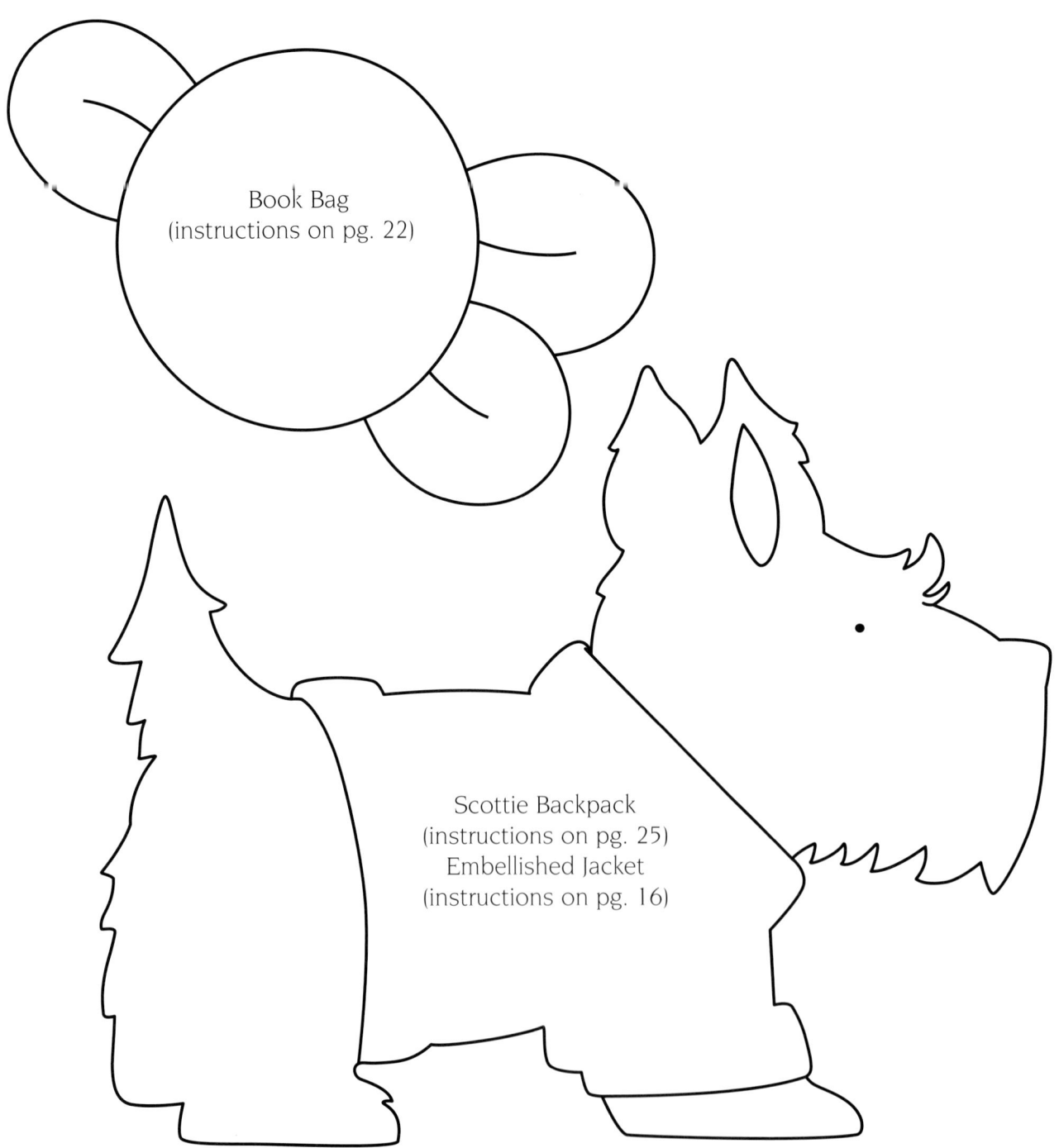

Book Bag
(instructions on pg. 22)

Scottie Backpack
(instructions on pg. 25)
Embellished Jacket
(instructions on pg. 16)

Mary Engelbreit Enterprises, Inc., and Leisure Arts, Inc., grant permission to the owner of this book to copy or trace the patterns on this page for personal use only.

Mary Engelbreit Enterprises, Inc., and Leisure Arts, Inc., grant permission to the owner of this book to copy or trace the patterns on this page for personal use only.

29

Me & My Home

Give your home the air of a cozy cottage with a few very "Mary" touches! Plump pillows and a cheery rug add a dash of whimsy to any space, while an enchanting chair cover, table skirt, and wall hanging dress up a room in the most delightful way!

Heart Pillow

You will need ½ yd Mary Engelbreit flower fabric; ¼ yd yellow checked fabric; red, green, and yellow felt; red, green, and yellow embroidery floss; tracing paper; freezer paper; and polyester fiberfill.

Match right sides and use a ½" seam allowance for all sewing unless otherwise indicated.

1. Read **General Instructions**, pages 42-44.
2. Enlarge half heart pattern, page 41, 116% on photocopier. Trace pattern onto tracing paper. Turn tracing paper over, align dashed line, and trace pattern again to complete heart. Use pattern to cut two hearts from flower fabric for pillow front and back.
3. For ruffle, cut two 4" wide selvage-to-selvage strips from yellow fabric. Sew short ends together to form one long strip; trim to 79". Sew remaining short ends together to form a loop. Matching wrong sides, press loop in half lengthwise.
4. Baste ⅜" and ¼" from raw edges of ruffle. Pull basting threads to gather ruffle to fit pillow front, distributing gathers evenly; baste in place.
5. Leaving an opening for turning, sew pillow back to pillow front. Clip curves and turn pillow right side out; press.
6. Stuff pillow with fiberfill; hand sew opening closed.
7. Trace one flower center and two of each flower and leaf pattern piece, page 40, onto freezer paper. Iron shiny side of freezer paper pattern to felt with warm iron. Cut out felt along outside pattern lines. Backstitch vein lines on leaves with green floss. Remove freezer paper.
8. Blanket stitch leaf pieces together with green floss. Baste leaves to back of one flower, positioning them as shown. Blanket stitch flower center to front of the same flower with yellow floss. Blanket stitch flower pieces together with red floss. Where leaves are attached, blanket stitch both top and bottom of flower. Remove basting.
9. Tack flower on pillow as shown.

Bolster Pillow

You will need ½ yd Mary Engelbreit white cherry fabric; ⅓ yd Mary Engelbreit black cherry fabric; scraps of solid red, solid brown, and green print fabrics; scrap of batting; 1⅛ yds red jumbo rickrack; 1¼ yds of ¾"w red polka-dot grosgrain ribbon; 13" x 18" bolster pillow form; tracing paper; freezer paper; and fabric glue.

Match right sides and use a ½" seam allowance for all sewing unless otherwise indicated.

1. Read **General Instructions**, pages 42-44.
2. Cut a 10½" x 19" rectangle of black fabric. Cut two 13" x 19" rectangles of white fabric. Matching long edges, sew one white rectangle to black fabric. Sew remaining white rectangle to remaining long edge of black fabric.
3. Cut two 19" lengths of rickrack; glue in place along seams.
4. Press remaining long edge of each white rectangle 5½" to wrong side; topstitch. Fold sewn piece in half lengthwise; sew.
5. Turn right side out. Insert pillow form.
6. Cut two 22" lengths of ribbon; wrap one length around each end of pillow and tie into a bow.
7. Use leaf pattern on page 40 and refer to **Making Shapes**, page 43, to make one leaf from green fabric.
8. Trace stem and circle patterns, page 40, and cut out. Cut one stem from brown fabric. Cut two circles from solid red fabric for yo-yo cherries.
9. To make each yo-yo cherry, use matching thread to sew running stitches around entire circle ⅛" from edge. With right side of fabric facing out, pull thread to tightly gather fabric; knot thread to secure. Flatten yo-yo so that gathered circle is at the center.
10. Glue stem, leaf, and cherries in place on one end of bolster pillow.

Chair Cover

For each chair cover, you will need a straight-backed chair, newspaper, black polka-dot fabric (amount will depend on size of chair; see Steps 2-6), $1/2$ yd black striped fabric, $1/8$ yd yellow checked fabric, $1/4$ yd solid red fabric, $1/3$ yd green print fabric, freezer paper, $1/4$ yd batting, and a hot glue gun.

Match right sides and use a $1/2$" seam allowance for all sewing unless otherwise indicated.

1. Read **General Instructions**, pages 42-44.
2. Follow **Fig. 1** to measure across front of chair seat (A) and across back of chair seat (B); measure depth of chair seat (C). Use these measurements to draw pattern for chair seat on newspaper; draw a second line $1/2$" outside the first. Cut out pattern on outside line. Use pattern to cut one piece from polka-dot fabric for chair seat.

Fig. 1

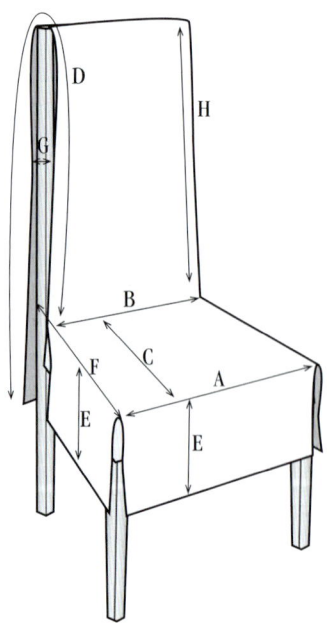

3. For chair back cover, measure from back of chair seat, over back of chair and down to bottom of desired skirt length (D); add 1". Measure across back of chair seat (B); add 1". Cut a piece of polka-dot fabric the determined measurements.
4. For front skirt piece, measure desired length of the skirt (E) and add 1". Measure across front of chair seat (A); add 1". Cut a piece of polka-dot fabric the determined measurements.
5. For side skirt pieces, measure the desired length of skirt (E) and add 1". Measure along side of chair seat, including the thickness of the chair back (F); add 1". Cut two pieces of polka-dot fabric the determined measurements.
6. For chair back insets, measure the thickness of the chair back (G); add 1". Measure the height from the chair seat to the top of the chair back (H); add 1". Cut two pieces of polka-dot fabric the determined measurements.
7. To make hems, press raw edges $1/4$" to wrong side; press $1/4$" to wrong side again and stitch in place. Hem one short edge of chair back cover piece. Hem both short edges and one long edge of each skirt piece.
8. Matching right sides and raw edges, stitch chair back cover to back of chair seat cover; stitch front skirt piece to front of chair seat cover.
9. Place cover on chair. On both sides, place a pin where chair back cover folds over thickness of chair back (**Fig. 2**). Remove cover from chair.

Fig. 2

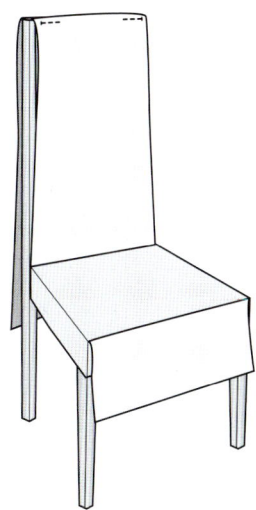

10. Lay chair back cover flat. Matching right sides and raw edges, place chair back inset along side of chair back cover so that the short edge of inset is $1/2$" above pin. Sew in place. Clip chair back cover at pin; pivot and stretch cover to turn corner of inset. Continue matching raw edges and sew in place. Repeat to clip and pivot at last corner; sew remaining long edge of inset in place.
11. Repeat to sew remaining inset to remaining long edge of chair back cover.
12. Stitch side pieces to sides of chair seat cover. Press.
13. For sash, cut two 8" wide selvage-to-selvage strips of striped fabric. Sew strips together along short edges and trim to 67" long. Fold strip in half lengthwise. Fold in half widthwise and trim ends at an angle; unfold widthwise.
14. Leaving an opening for turning, sew long edges and short sides of strip together. Clip corners and turn right side out; press. Hand sew opening closed.
15. Using pattern on page 39 and making each color a separate shape (leaves should be one big piece with round center), refer to **Making Shapes**, page 43, to make three flower and leaf sets.
16. Glue one flower to each leaf set and one flower center to each flower. Arrange flower sets as shown in photo and glue together.
17. Tie sash around chair with ends hanging in back. Hand sew flowers to sash.

Table Skirt

You will need a round decorator table, Mary Engelbreit yellow cherry fabric, Mary Engelbreit flower fabric, red checked fabric, black striped fabric (amounts of all fabrics will depend on size of table; see Steps 2-4), string, fabric marking pen, thumbtack, red ball fringe, various $1/2$" - $3/4$" dia. black buttons, red rickrack, and clear nylon thread.

Match right sides and use a $1/2$" seam allowance for all sewing unless otherwise indicated.

1. Read **General Instructions**, pages 42-44.
2. Measure the diameter of table; add 2". Cut a square of yellow fabric using this measurement.
3. Add 1" to table diameter. Refer to **Cutting a Fabric Circle**, page 43, and use this measurement for string to cut circle from fabric square for top of skirt.
4. For skirt length measurement, multiply table diameter times five. For width measurement, measure from height of table to floor; subtract $13 1/2$". Piecing as needed, cut a strip of yellow fabric the determined measurements.
5. Cut a $3 1/2$" wide strip of red fabric the determined skirt length; sew to yellow fabric along one long edge.
6. Multiply length measurement from Step 4 by 1.5. Cut a 7" wide strip of floral fabric and a 5" wide strip of striped fabric this length. Cut rickrack to determined length.

7. Sew floral and striped fabrics together along one long edge.
8. Baste $3/8$" and $1/4$" from long raw edge of floral fabric. Pull basting threads to gather ruffle to long raw edge of red fabric, distributing gathers evenly; sew in place.
9. Fold table skirt widthwise and sew, matching fabric seams, to form a tube.
10. Baste $3/8$" and $1/4$" from raw edge of yellow fabric. Pull basting threads to gather ruffle to top of skirt, distributing gathers evenly; sew in place around top of skirt.
11. Multiply diameter of table by 3.14; cut ball fringe this length. Use clear nylon thread to sew fringe on seam between skirt and top of skirt; sew rickrack between bottom two sections of skirt.
12. Sew black buttons as desired to red checked section of skirt.
13. Hem bottom of table skirt $1/2$" to wrong side.

Wall Hanging

You will need $3/8$ yd red polka-dot fabric, $1/3$ yd blue print fabric, $1/8$ yd green print fabric, $1/8$ yd yellow checked fabric, $1 1/4$ yds of $7/8$"w black and white checked ribbon, $1 1/4$ yds yellow rickrack, four $7/8$" dia. yellow buttons, $1 1/2$ yds of $1 1/2$"w black polka-dot satin ribbon, tracing paper, transfer paper, paper-backed fusible web, yellow thread, fabric glue, and a black fine-tip permanent marker.

1. Read **General Instructions**, pages 42-44.
2. Cut two 12" squares of red fabric and a 12" square of fusible web. Iron fusible web to back of one fabric square. Remove paper backing and fuse to back of remaining square. Trim fused fabric to 11" square.
3. Cut a 10" square of blue fabric and a 10" square of fusible web. Iron fusible web to back of fabric; trim to 9" square. Center and fuse blue fabric square to red square.
4. Cut four 10" lengths of checked ribbon. Arrange ribbon lengths along each side of blue square. Glue side ribbons in place. Miter ends of remaining ribbon by cutting diagonally from outside corner of ribbon to inside corner of ribbon square. Glue remaining ribbons in place.
5. Arrange and glue yellow rickrack around outside edges of glued ribbons.
6. Use pattern on page 39 and refer to **Preparing Fusible Appliqués**, page 42, to prepare flower, flower center, and leaves. Arrange flower pieces on blue square as shown in photo; fuse in place. Draw over embellishment lines and outline of flower, flower center, and leaves with permanent marker.
7. Loop yellow thread through holes on each button; glue in place on back of button. Glue one button to each corner of blue square.
8. Tie polka-dot ribbon into a bow with approximately $3 1/4$" loops. Cut each ribbon end at an angle. Arrange wall hanging to lay flat on ends of ribbon; glue in place.

Looped Rug

You will need a 24" x 30" piece of 3.75 mesh rug canvas, 20" x 30" piece of cardboard, latch hook, 1 3/4 yds solid black fabric, 1 3/4 yds solid white fabric, 3/4 yd green print fabric, 7/8 yd solid red fabric, 1/8 yd yellow checked fabric, 3 3/8 yds blue print fabric, rotary cutter, rotary cutting mat, black permanent pen, and clear tape.

1. Read **General Instructions**, pages 42-44.
2. Cut canvas to 18 1/2" x 28 1/2". Place canvas on cardboard. Measure in 1/2" around edges of canvas; mark with pen. Mark another line 2 1/2" in from first. In between these lines, mark off 2 1/2" squares.
3. Copy pattern on page 39 three times. Lay copies between canvas and cardboard, arranging flowers as shown in photo. Tape copies in place on cardboard. Trace flowers and leaves with pen. Remove canvas from cardboard.
4. Use rotary cutter and mat to cut each fabric into 3/4" wide selvage-to-selvage strips. Cut each strip into ten 4" lengths.
5. As you hook the outside edge, fold the 1/2" of extra canvas to the back and hook through both layers of canvas. To keep canvas square, begin at one corner on the top or bottom of the canvas. Work across the row, changing strip colors as necessary, before moving to the next row. Fabric yardages given are based on the hooking pattern shown (**Fig. 1**). Use this hooking pattern to ensure having enough yardage to complete the project.

Fig. 1

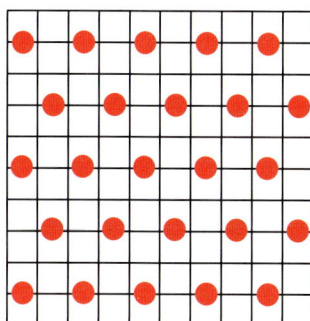

7. Leaving shaft of hook in loop, catch ends of strip in hook and pull them through the loop (**Fig. 3**). Pull knot tight (**Fig. 4**).

Fig. 3   Fig. 4

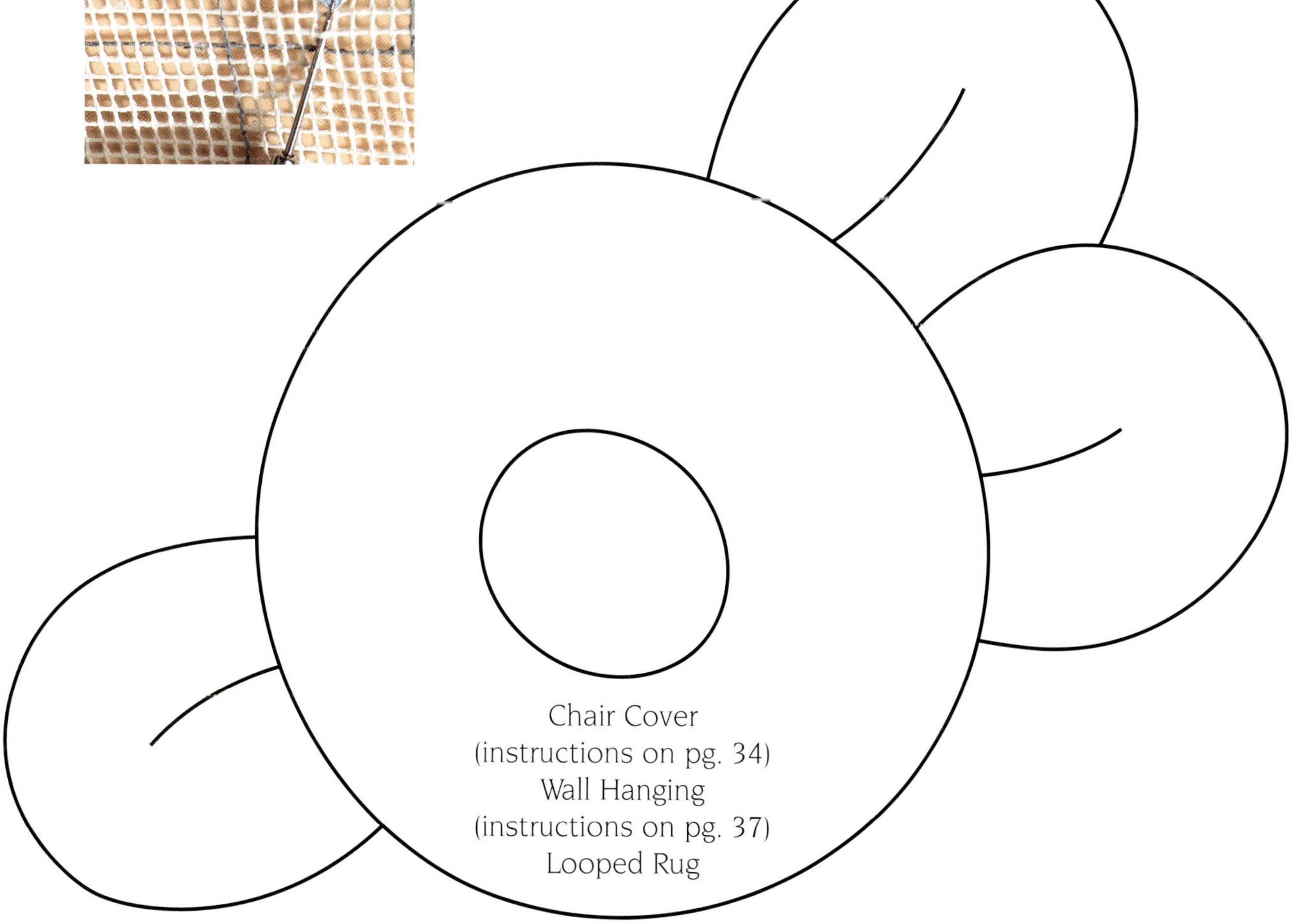

6. To hook fabric onto canvas, slide hook beneath one crossbar in canvas. Wrap one fabric strip around hook with ends even (**Fig. 2**); slide hook back through canvas until strip is about halfway through.

Fig. 2

Chair Cover
(instructions on pg. 34)
Wall Hanging
(instructions on pg. 37)
Looped Rug

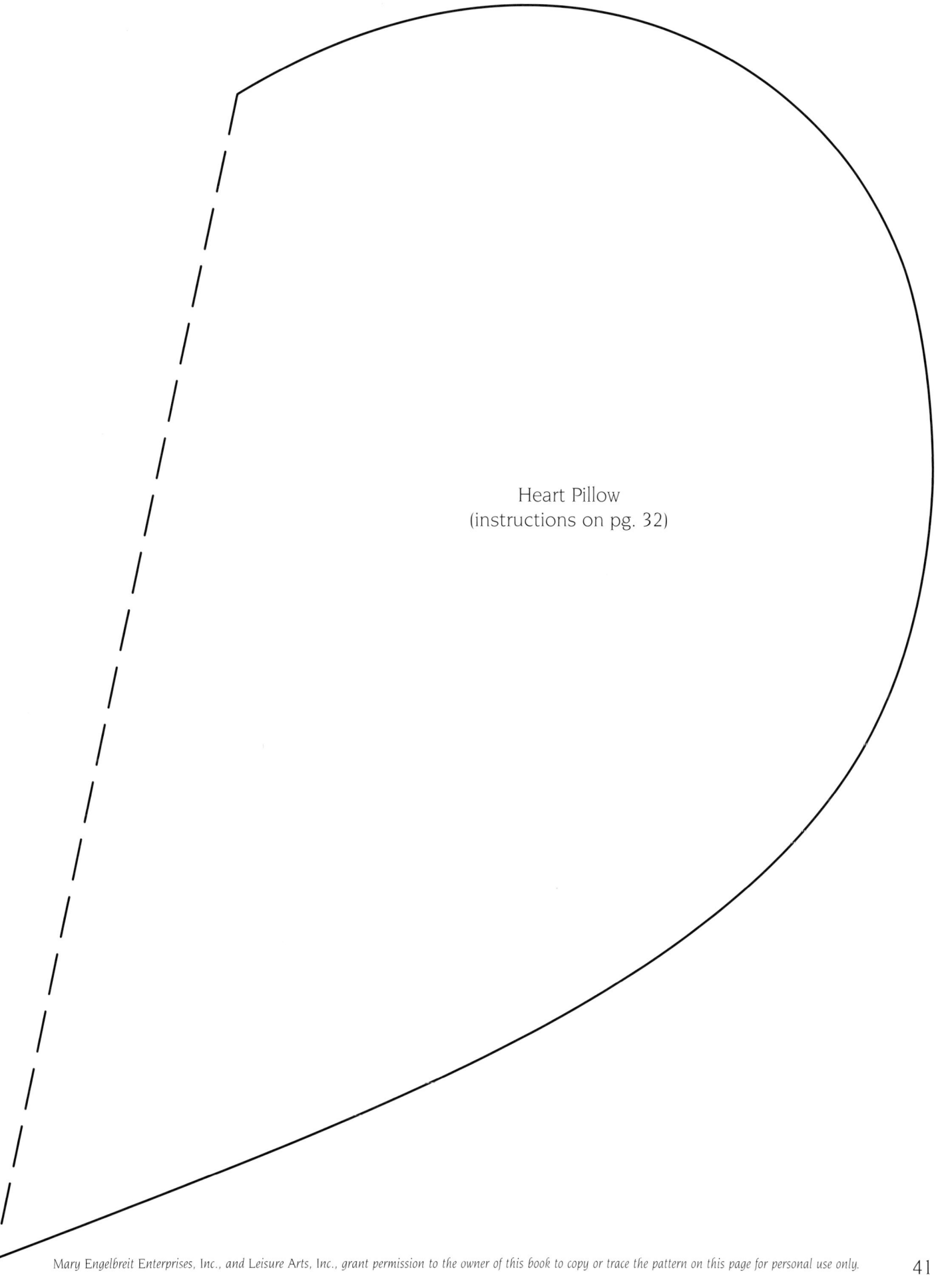

Heart Pillow
(instructions on pg. 32)

General Instructions

Preparing Fusible Appliqués

1. Trace pattern onto tracing paper; cut out. Turn traced pattern over to reverse pattern. Leaving 1/2" between pieces, draw around each pattern piece onto paper side of fusible web as many times as indicated in project instructions.
2. Follow manufacturer's instructions to fuse drawn patterns to wrong side of fabric. Do not remove paper backing. Cut out appliqué pieces along drawn lines.
3. To transfer embellishment lines from your tracing paper pattern, place transfer paper, coated side down, on right side of appliqué. Place tracing paper pattern over transfer paper and draw over detail lines with ballpoint pen that does not write or dull pencil.
4. Remove paper backing from appliqué pieces.

Machine Satin Stitching

1. Thread needle of sewing machine. Set sewing machine for a medium width zigzag stitch (approximately 1/8") and a very short stitch length. Set upper tension slightly looser than for regular stitching.
2. Beginning on as straight an edge as possible, position fabric so that most of the satin stitching will be on the appliqué piece. Do not backstitch; hold upper thread toward you and sew over it two or three stitches to anchor thread. Following Steps 3-6 for stitching corners and curves, stitch over exposed raw edges of appliqué pieces.
3. (Dots on Figs. indicate where to leave needle in fabric when pivoting.) For **outside corners**, stitch 1/8" past the corner, stopping with the needle in **background** fabric (**Fig. 1**). Raise presser foot. Pivot project, lower presser foot, and stitch adjacent side (**Fig. 2**).

Fig. 1   Fig. 2

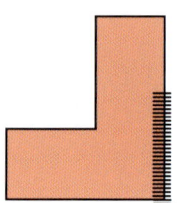 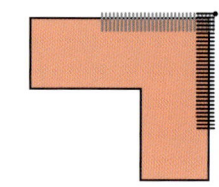

4. For **inside corners**, stitch 1/8" past the corner, stopping with the needle in the **appliqué** fabric (**Fig. 3**). Raise presser foot. Pivot project, lower presser foot, and stitch adjacent side (**Fig. 4**).

Fig. 3   Fig. 4

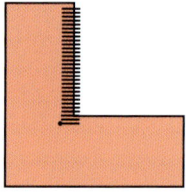 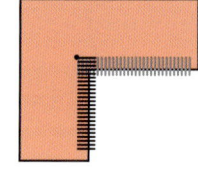

5. When stitching **outside curves**, stop with needle in **background** fabric. Raise presser foot and pivot project as needed. Lower presser foot and continue stitching, pivoting as often as necessary to follow curve (**Fig. 5**).

Fig. 5

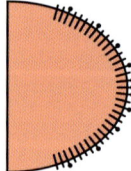

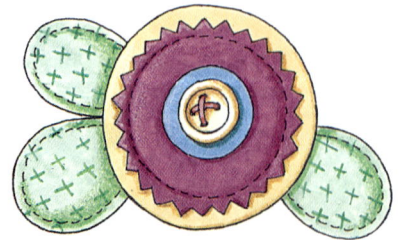

6. When stitching **inside curves**, stop with needle in **appliqué** fabric. Raise presser foot and pivot project as needed. Lower presser foot and continue stitching, pivoting as often as necessary to follow curve (**Fig. 6**).

Fig. 6

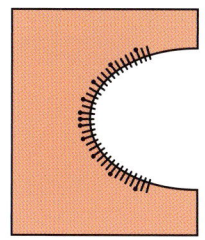

7. Do not backstitch at end of stitching. Pull threads to wrong side of background fabric; knot thread and trim ends.

Making Shapes

1. Trace patterns onto freezer paper. For each freezer paper pattern, cut two squares of fabric and one square of batting large enough to fit pattern. Iron shiny side of freezer paper pattern to wrong side of one fabric square with warm iron. With pattern on top, layer fabric squares, right sides together, on batting.
2. Machine stitch around freezer paper pattern. Peel off freezer paper and trim fabric and batting $1/4$" from stitching line. Cutting through **only** one layer of fabric, cut a small slash in the fabric side of sewn piece. Clip curves and turn. Machine stitch embellishment lines if needed. Glue opening closed.

Cutting a Fabric Circle

1. Matching right sides, fold fabric square in half from top to bottom and again from left to right.
2. Tie one end of a length of string to a fabric marking pen. Measuring from pen, insert a thumbtack through string at length indicated in project instructions. Insert thumbtack through folded corner of fabric. Holding tack in place and keeping string taut, mark cutting line (**Fig. 7**).

Fig. 7

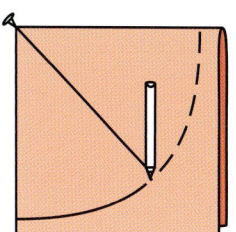

Making Bias Strips

1. Fold fabric square in half diagonally; cut on fold to make two triangles.
2. With right sides together and using a $1/4$" seam allowance, sew triangles together (**Fig. 8**). Press seam allowances open.

Fig. 8

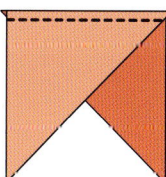

3. On wrong side of fabric, draw lines the width specified in the project instructions, parallel to long edges (**Fig. 9**). Cut off any remaining fabric less than this width.

   Fig. 9

   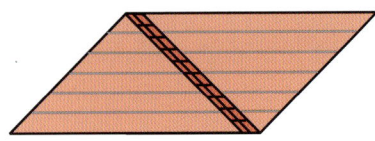

4. Mark seamlines ¼" from short edges of fabric (**Fig. 10**).

   Fig. 10

   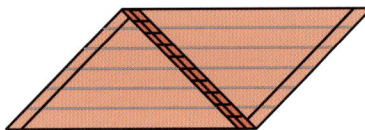

5. With right sides inside, match short raw edges so that first drawn line of section on top meets second drawn line of section on bottom. Insert pins through drawn lines at the point where drawn lines intersect, making sure the pins go through intersections on both sides (**Fig. 11**). Using a ¼" seam allowance, sew edges together. Press seam allowances open.

   Fig. 11

   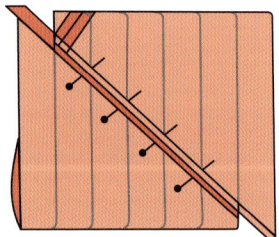

6. To cut a continuous strip, begin cutting along first drawn line (**Fig. 12**). Continue cutting along drawn line around tube.

   Fig. 12

   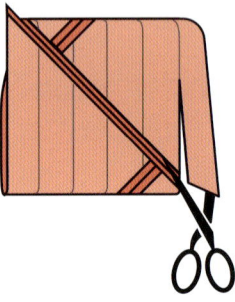

7. Trim each end of bias strip as shown in **Fig. 13**.

   Fig. 13

   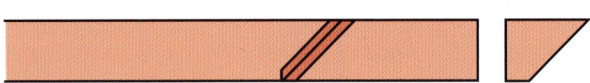

Embroidering

Use three strands of embroidery floss for all stitching unless otherwise indicated in project instructions. Follow the stitch diagrams to bring the needle up at odd numbers and down at even numbers.

BLANKET STITCH   **BACKSTITCH**

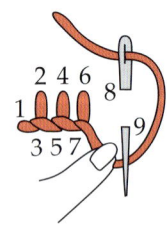   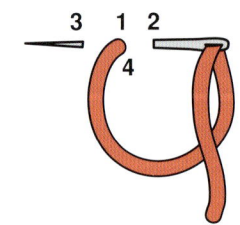

RUNNING STITCH

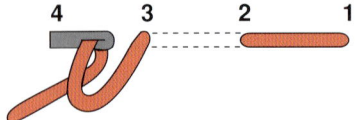